Basics of Successful Agriculture in the Tropics

Basic guideline for sustainable, ecological, organic gardening in tropical and subtropical climates

1st edition: Dr. Oliver Pfaff (January.2016). **Basics of successful agriculture in the tropics,** Create Space Edition.

2nd expanded edition: Dr. Oliver Pfaff (May.2016). **Basics of successful agriculture in the tropics,** Create Space Edition.

3rd expanded and complemented edition: Dr. Oliver Pfaff (July.2020). **Basics of successful agriculture in the tropics,** Create Space Edition.

Edited by Jessica Cronin, M.A.
www.thereadersblock.com
jesscronin23@gmail.com

ISBN-13: 978-1523813506 (CreateSpace-Assigned)
ISBN-10: 1523813504

Table of contents:
The Basics of Successful, Sustainable, Ecological, Organic Agriculture in the Tropics
Introduction:
Basic Requirements:
A. **Soil with enough organic matter**
B. **Clean water for proper supply**
C. **General rules**
1. The soil should never be 'naked' and exposed to direct sunlight
2. The soil should always be covered
3. Sealing of the soil should be avoided
4. Light sensitive plants should be shaded
5. The soil should be organized in furrows or terraces
6. The soil should never be under stagnant water long-term
7. The soil should be checked for its composition and its pH. Deviations and deficiencies should be corrected, if necessary
8. You should always mix different plants in clusters or rows; try companion planting and crop rotation

9. You should always have leguminous plants in your plant assortment
10. Give the plants enough space and sunlight
11. The fertilizers used should be from a natural source

How to fertilize?

12. Apply vermiculture
13. Produce your own BIOL
14. Create a fishpond to produce your own liquid fertilizer
15. All organic waste material should be used to create humus. Create a compost heap
16. Create an intelligent irrigating system
17. Irrigate the plants in the morning and / or evening hours
18. Grow according to the necessities of the plants
19. Protect your plantings with windbreak and hedge trees
20. When you eliminate plants, replace them with others
21. Prune plants and trees extensively
22. Use natural pest control
23. Install beehives
24. Try Electro-culture

THE BASICS OF SUCCESSFUL, SUSTAINABLE, ECOLOGICAL, ORGANIC AGRICULTURE IN THE TROPICS

Introduction:

The drive for yield optimization generally leads to the massive use of herbicides and pesticides in modern agriculture. The long-term effect is continuous soil degradation, which, at the end, demands an ever rising need for fertilizers. Product quality suffers from these techniques, and income shrinks due to high production costs. Still, this kind of agriculture is efficiently promoted by the companies offering chemical solutions, but the growing resistance of plagues and the rising need for fertilizers make it increasingly less attractive. Especially, small farmers have to suffer the consequences of rising production costs and competing with industrialized agriculture.

This brochure aims at collecting basic data about an approach to sustainable, ecological, organic agriculture in tropical and subtropical climates, and to provide a guideline for interested gardeners and small farmers. This compiled information even may serve as a blueprint for a new concept of sustainable, agricultural production. We may call it SUSTAINABLE ECOLOGICAL ORGANIC AGRICULTURE (SEOA).

The focus is on healthy soil and plant management, which provides the basis for a relatively lower cost and higher quality harvest, and, thus, offers not only a sustainable business while conserving resources, but also a better income.

Although this booklet doesn't focus on commercial aspects and is for self-sufficient, amateur gardeners with a self-catering mentality rather than for farmers with hundreds of hectares, everyone can pick out something from the basic rules and ideas described in this brochure and apply it according to his circumstances.

Perhaps, this way, each one of us can contribute, by his means, to create safe and valuable food production. Another aspect is the creation of a better quality of life for ourselves and those working with us. Thus, each one can contribute to make at least his little share of the world a bit better.

In India a whole state (Kerala) went organic, with thousands of small farmers producing healthy food in self-sustainable conditions. Bhutan, a small kingdom in the Himalaya, has banned all agrochemicals such as pesticides, herbicides and even artificial fertilizers.

It is possible, and this booklet is intended to give hints and to show how.

In the following, you will find the basic information (Chapters A and B) about the two essential means and basic requirements for successful, sustainable, ecological, organic agriculture: about **SOIL and WATER**

The quality of both has to be as good as possible in order to have positive results at the beginning without the use of chemicals and artificial fertilizer. With the time, applying the ideas mentioned in the chapters to follow, you should expect positive results consistently.

The soil quality can be improved continuously, whereas the water quality depends mostly on local circumstances. Nevertheless, its quality can be improved by simple means, like filters or additives.

Thereafter, in Chapter C, you will find point-by-point (points 1 through 26) the most important laws of successful, ecological, organic gardening, without the claim of being complete.

At the end of this section, I have added a special issue you should consider. Try to work in harmony with the rhythms of nature, such as the phases of the moon. Old farming rules very often serve as viable empiric decision maker. This point can be part of your stable success if you apply the basic rules mentioned. Listen around and make your own experiences with its use.

In Section D, you will find a list of the basic tools you need to be able to manage a small, ecological, organic operation.

After the lecture, you will have a lot of new ideas and, probably, even more questions. Take a diary and start to create your own collection of ideas and experiences to design your own individual strategy.

Basic Requirements:

A. Soil with enough organic matter

Whenever you go through a forest, or pass along some wasteland, you can observe abundant and diverse plant growth although, obviously, nobody is fertilizing there. Nature itself takes care of this by creating soil fertility, recycling all self-produced organic matter, and keeping the nutrients in continuous recovery. A tree takes the nutrient elements from the earth and turns them into leaves that, at a point in time, turn brown and fall to the earth, forming a layer on top of last year's already largely decomposed leaves. Just a few centimeters below the fallen leaves, we find a sweet-smelling layer of composted leaf humus, inhabited by an infinite number of microorganisms.

To create such healthy soil is the task of the farmer who wants to avoid, largely, artificial means in his crop production.

The productivity and fertility of the farm, and plant resistance to pests and disease, depends largely on the quality of the soil. Soil is always a mixture of inorganic and organic matter in different compositions, whereby the ratio of the components varies a lot. There are stones, gravel, sand or clay as the inorganic part, and triturated, partly rotten organic matter, from trunks to twigs and leaves, and all the tiny organic particles that you can observe floating up when the soil gets mixed with water in a transparent glass. These are the particles that allow soil microorganisms to live, and they use them to prepare readily available, nutritive compounds for the plants.

If this organic part lacks, there is no habitat for soil microorganisms, and, thus, the soil is poor in nutrients and only serves as a means for the anchoring of the plant roots.

The richer in organic matter, the more fertile and healthy, in the sense of agricultural use, is the soil, usually.

We are not to forget that, in the tropics, the formation of soil is somehow different from the process of soil formation in regions with frost and freezing temperatures. The crushing of inorganic material is faster in cold regions, whereas the degradation and decomposition of organic matter is accelerated in the tropics.

There are basically three different soil types we distinguish. Your soil is just a combination of these three types of weathered rock particles-sand, silt, and clay-plus the additional, and essential, fourth element: the organic particles.

The composition of the inorganic soil components can be detected according to the soil pyramid below. The size of the inorganic particles is the measure, where sand is the biggest and clay is the smallest.

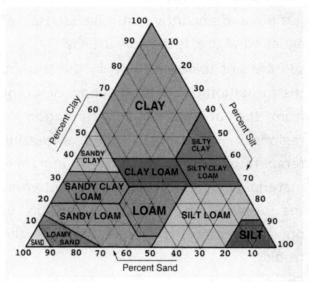

USDA textural triangle

The graph shows the possible inorganic soil compositions, whereby loam is the term for the most desirable composition for agriculture. It is an ideal mix of the three basic components.

Just follow the lines showing the percentages of each side of the triangle representing one of the three components and, at the cross point, you end up with your specific composition of inorganic soil particles.

Apart from rocks and gravel, which can be present in all of the soil types, sand is the largest particle in the soil. When you rub it between your fingers it feels rather rough, due to its particle size and its sharp edges. Sand doesn't hold water long-term and cannot hold many nutrients.

Silt is a soil particle whose size is between that of sand and clay. Silt feels smooth and powdery, and, when it is wet, it feels smooth but not sticky. It leaves dirt on your skin when you roll it between your fingers. It holds water and nutrients better than sand, without becoming boggy.

Clay is the smallest of the inorganic soil particles. Clay is silky when dry and sticky when wet. Soils high in clay content are called heavy soils. Clay can hold a lot of nutrients, but it compacts easily and is poor in oxygen and gets boggy when it is not well drained.

Depending on the inorganic soil composition, and its gravel and rock admixture, you either have a light and sandy soil poor in nutrients, a heavy, cloggy and dense, nutrient rich, clay-like soil, or anything in between.

Each extreme soil type is favored by certain plant life. As you want to plant different vegetables, crops and fruit, you should try to create, in the course of the time, a healthy mix of the three components and enrich them with enough organic matter.

Water and air will fill the spaces that remain empty between the organic and inorganic particles of various sizes, the soil pores. A heavy, loamy soil contains few, and very small, pores for air and space for root development and should be improved by adding sand. However, extremely sandy soils can't keep water and nutrients for much time, and should be enriched by adding smaller inorganic and organic particles.

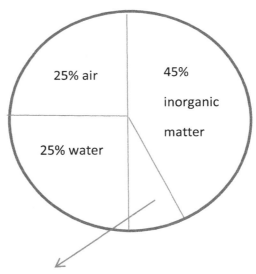

25% air

45% inorganic matter

25% water

5% organic matter

This is how the composition of a healthy soil structure should look.

The organic part of the ground serves as food for the soil microorganisms, which, by metabolizing organic matter, create compounds of phosphorus, nitrogen and potassium accessible for plant life. Around one-third of all species live in the soil, promoting soil fertility by their metabolic action.

An easy way to test the composition of the soil, roughly, is to mix a spoonful of it in a transparent glass with water. The inorganic compounds usually sink to the ground, whereas organic matter floats to the top. In this way, you can check the different sizes of the inorganic and the organic particles composing your soil and establish certain percentages. This helps you to see the changes in composition when you start to add lacking compounds and build up the humus by appropriate means.

Another, more sophisticated way of investigating the percentage of humus is by burning the completely dry soil in a crucible with a Bunsen burner after weighing it. Under the heat, it will turn red and smell like burnt hair or fingernails. The loss in weight after this procedure is equivalent to the completely burnt organic matter.

One of the main reasons why your soil loses organic matter is consumption without replacement, as well as erosion. So, the rain washes away the valuable small organic particles and leaves, basically, just the heavier ones, sand and stones.

Another factor is wind, which blows away superficial humus particles when the soil is uncovered and dry, without adequate wind shielding hedges or growth.

National Geographic revealed in its December 2015 edition that, from 1960 until today, one-third of arable land has been lost due to erosion. The knowledge that the natural buildup of fertile land needs centuries, and can be destroyed within minutes, should create more consciousness, at least amongst farmers, to look after their soil carefully.

This is why many fields look stony. It happens especially where soil is uncovered with plant life.

But, still, the most important and initially mentioned reason is excessive agriculture, which exploits the soil and leads to a negative humus balance. More organic matter is consumed by the plants that grow in the field than is replaced.

Nature needs at least 500 years to build up a healthy humus soil mix, whereas exploiting farming methods can exhaust the soil within just a few decades. Also, flash floods and windstorms, as already mentioned above, may have this destructive, erosive effect within minutes.

The average percentage of organic matter varies usually between 2-6%. Very poor loamy or sandy soils have even less than 2% of organic-carbon matter, and very dark and rich soils have more than 8% of organic-carbon matter. Heavy, rich soils might have up to 18% of organic material. Such a high, or an even higher organic content, tends to make the soils boggy. Peat represents a special kind of soil, because it usually consists of almost 100% organic matter.

There are some main functions that organic matter promotes in the soil:

- It is the source of food and nutrients for soil organisms and plants.
- It promotes a wide range of life in the soil.
- It improves soil structure.
- It helps regulate water absorption and drainage.
- It provides storage space for plant nutrients in the soil.

In Sustainable Ecological Organic Agriculture (SEOA) the humus balance should be at least even, but a positive humus balance is even better. Aim for raising the percentage of organic matter in the soil to values around at least 5%, which is more difficult in warm tropical climates than in temperate climate zones, due to faster turnover and decay of organic material. This is one of the reasons why we find, in the Amazonian rainforest, only a very thin layer of humus on mainly stony and sandy subsoil.

Natural fertility doesn't depend directly on heavily promoted organic material itself, but on the soil organisms, starting with earthworms and insects and ending with an endless army of fungi and bacteria, living on the organic material and creating the organic-mineral compounds that nurture plant life.

In summary, an ideal soil for agriculture should be a diverse mix of differently shaped and sized organic and inorganic particles that create a light structure with enough pore space for air and water. The clinging together of these soil particles creates the aggregation state of the soil, defining its structure and stability.

The aggregation state of the soil particles is very important for its stability against erosion, and also for nutrient and water retention, amongst others. This aggregation, to a big extent, is promoted by the soil bacteria, forming sticky, gelatin-like biofilms which paste the particles together. Fungi add their net-like mycelium to hold everything together. Some mycorrhizal fungi create hyphae, coated and glued together with Glomalin, a natural, water resistant super glue. This prevents nutrient loss in the fungi and creates soil aggregates by gluing together and stabilizing the particles. .

Plants reach optimum growth in soil with a stable, diverse and light structure and a good aggregation, inhabited by plenty of microorganisms.

An improvement of the soil quality, by raising the humus content of the soil, leads to an increase of soil life, and thus, its fertility. There are billions of bacteria, millions of protozoa and fungi, and thousands of algae in just one tablespoon of healthy garden soil.

This is why an improvement of the soil quality, by raising the humus content, usually leads, due to the facts already described above, to the following positive effects:

- an increase in the aggregate stability and an improvement of the soil structure
- an increase in pore volume and, thus, an improvement in the water holding and filter capacity of the soil
- an increase in the biological activity of the soil microorganisms

- a reduction of the susceptibility to erosion
- an increase of nutrient exchange capacity
- an increase of the promotion of metabolic processes in the plants and activation of healthy rooting
- a reduction of the susceptibility of the plants to disease
- an increase in the mycorrhization (growth of decomposing fungi) and an improvement in nutrient transfer
- stronger biological control against pathogens and plagues
- higher yields and, thus, more income security with an increase up to 30%
- an increase in the flavor quality of the products
- a reduction in nitrate content, an increase of value-adding ingredients in the final product, and an improvement in shelf life

Note: Soil, by itself, is a very fascinating and vast topic that could fill a whole book.

A book, called "Fertile Soil is not just Dirt", about the basics of soil science, dedicated to make soil science easy to understand for everybody interested in this field, I published on May 2018.

B. Clean water for proper supply

Water means life, water means growth, and water means healthy production. However, water can also mean destruction of harvest and putrefaction of fruit and vegetables, if not applied properly.

Water is the essential link between organic cells and the nutrients they need for their metabolism. In plants, the water, called xylem, transports inorganic and organic nutrients from the roots to the leaves, whereas, as phloem, it distributes the products of photosynthesis into the different organs of the plant.

Water is able to do this because of its extraordinary properties as a universal solvent. This implies that the quality of water is an important factor in order to have healthy plant growth. Water can look clear and may taste clean, but this is not a criteria for water quality; its quality depends largely on the composition of dissolved trace elements and hidden contamination you cannot see or taste.

If the water, for example, is contaminated with heavy metals or pesticides, it may have a long-term diseasing effect for the plants themselves, and, also, for the consumers of those products.

Nevertheless, the most important factor to be considered is the salinity of the water. Salts are usually dissolved in small quantities, but continuous soil irrigation and evaporation of water, especially by furrow irrigation, can lead to an accumulation of salts in the soil to a damaging extent. It also leads to less fertile soil. Higher levels of salinity (too much sodium chloride accumulated in the soil) and sodicity (too much sodium accumulated in the soil) not only influence the chemical and physical characteristics of soils, but also greatly affect soil microbial life, and its biochemical properties, negatively. Huge, once-blooming cotton fields around the Aral Sea are now salty deserts due to improper irrigation.

Basically, we have to avoid two things: lack of water and too much water. We have to be able to supply water, if necessary, from a safe and clean water supply, and we have to do everything to avoid stagnant water for too long.

Each plant species has a different water consumption scheme. There are plants that need much water, such as rice, or plants that need very little water, such as fig trees. Another fact we have to take into consideration is that plants have a different need for water in the course of their life cycle. For example, rice needs much water at the beginning and just little at the end.

As we need to adapt the planting scheme and the selection of the plants we grow based on our soil conditions, we need to adapt it also to the water supply and drainage possibilities in our plot of land. If we have an arid place, we need a safe water supply; if we have a wet sink, we have to create little drainage ditches and plant preferably on the mounds.

Depending on the local climate, and on the size of your piece of land, you might need an irrigation system. The best one consists of black, flexible plastic tubes with little dripping holes in the classic planting distances, called "soaker hoses". Either you put them below the surface or, like a snake, between the plants superficially. These tubes can be connected to a faucet or, even better, to an elevated water tank, where you can put additional liquid biologic preparations to strengthen or fertilize your plants whenever needed.

Of course, you should put only plants with a similar water requirement along each individual line, and not water your piece of land indiscriminately. This way you can irrigate your plants drop-wise very efficiently. You just have to decide which line to connect when and for how long. You can install these tubes permanently, or just for the time you find it necessary. Just take care, when you plow or dig over, not to damage your irrigating tubes.

Another way of irrigating is to let the water run along ditches prepared for watering (furrow irrigation). However, with this way, your water consumption is much higher, as well as is the danger of rising salt and sodium levels in your soil. Another difficulty is to add biologic additives to the water, because much of the material would be wasted in the furrows. This way of watering, in addition to the high consumption of water and other long-term, negative side effects, is usually only used in very remote, poor and still underdeveloped areas. Furrow irrigation, nowadays, is used to control the amount of water in paddy fields, or in the cultivation of some plants, like "Yautia de Coco" and others, that need moist soil.

If you irrigate with water sprinklers, you need quite a bit of pressure in the water pipe. You can use this way of irrigating especially for low-growing vegetables. In this case, you should preferably sprinkle in the evening, because you should avoid having water drops on leaves in the sun, which can act just like a burning glass singeing your leaves. Another reason to avoid daytime sprinkling is the possible difference between the temperature of the water and the sunlit leaves or soil, which can lead to some kind of temperature shock reaction.

It is a good idea to select an adequate irrigation system according to your possibilities and to your needs. In this case, plant the water-needy plants close to the faucet or well and plant the drought resistant plants at the far end of your site.

If your plot is hilly or is on a slope, usually the valleys are moist and the hilltops are drier. Choose your planting scheme accordingly.

A general rule is to avoid irrigating in the midday heat. Instead, you should irrigate in the morning and, especially, in the evening hours. Why, I will explain more closely in the further course of the book.

To irrigate, you should use pure well water from your own well, or, if this is not possible, water from a public line, if it is not treated with chlorine and iodine.

You are lucky if you have the possibility to create a water reservoir just for irrigation means, like a little pond, with or without fish, where the water can rest before being used, be it rainwater, well water or tap water.

A very good source of irrigation water can be the water of a fishpond or fish tank because it is already fertilizer enriched water whereby the fish excrements are broken down by nitrification bacteria into nitrates and nitrites in the soil. These are utilized by the plants as essential nutrients.

Another liquid enriched with natural fertilizer is the water from the drain of biodigestors or bio gas plants.

Remember: It is important, not only for sprinkling systems, to preferably irrigate in the morning hours, in the evening hours, or even at night time.

C. General rules:

1. The soil should never be 'naked' and exposed to direct sunlight.

The massive use of herbicides leads to the fatal destruction of soil-protecting natural growth. Erosion and soil depletion are two of the results. Another is the silent poisoning of the soil and its products, and consumers have to suffer the consequences at the end of the food chain.

Soil uncovered by plant life, wood chops, dry palm leaves or composting foil, and exposed to direct sunlight, suffers various impacts that lower its productivity and raise its humus loss.

On first hand, the superficial layers dry out easily, heat up and are exposed to destructive UV sunrays.

Because of this, microbiotic life diminishes in these layers considerably, as well as the healthy organic turnover and humus formation.

Wind and water can wash away precious superficial humus and soil layers and leave just dead and stony soil.

Also, uncovered soil doesn't produce any biomass that could contribute to the buildup of organic matter in the soil.

Today one person does the job to eliminate all wild growth in between the shrubs, plantains, and rows of crops with a 'poison pump' filled with herbicides on its back, which needed fifty years ago twenty workers to weed. Weeding needs to be done before the wild growth begins to form seeds and produces enough drying organic matter to over the soil, whereas herbicides mostly prevent the growth, so that the soil gets stripped of its natural protection.

2. The soil should always be covered.

Soil should always be covered by healthy plant growth, organic chops, leaves, composting foil, etc.- to keep moisture in the soil and to prevent overheating of the upper layer and overexposure to UV sunrays. This way, a suitable microclimate and healthy organic turnover and humus production, as well as healthy mycorrhization and microbiotic life, are guaranteed. This is necessary for the promotion of healthy plants and products.

It is always better to have continuous minimal growth of vegetation than bare soil. Of course, this controlled growth consumes nutrients. However, by cutting it continuously, it contributes, with the self-produced organic matter, to the buildup of humus. Above all, it also offers the environment for healthy microbiotic soil activity. If you use leguminous plants to cover the soil, you also have positive nitrogen supplementation due to rhizobiaceae, which live in symbiosis with the plants.

To avoid the uncontrolled growth of bad weeds, you can cover the soil in between your plantings with permeable foils, such as composting foil, that cover it while allowing transpiration of air and water. Or, you can use leaves from banana or palm trees to do the same job, adding additional organic matter to the soil after degradation.

Around the trunks of your fruit trees you should leave a circle with a diameter of about 1 m to 1,5 m free from growth of weeds or plants. You can leave this area uncovered or you can cover it with mulch or dried leafs. You even can raise the soil level on the outer border to make watering and the absorption of the rainwater in this area more efficient. Depending on the circumstances you can also sow beans or alfalfa or any other small leguminous species to help accumulate plant available nitrogen for the tree. This can even be done on slopes. You just cut the higher end of the circle and refill it below and stabilize it with stones or blocks.

3. Sealing of the soil should be avoided.

When the soil is uncovered, the baking sunlight after a rainfall very often creates a seal on the surface. This induces the water from the next rain to run off superficially, and the soil adsorbs less water than it could and should. This way, the soil loses its sponge-like function. This is one of the reasons why the superficial, hardened crust on the soil has to be broken up by a suitable tool, such as a hoe, cultivator or plow, every now and then. This should be done, preferably, during the moon phases that promote a desirable effect on the respective plant (see chapter 25 of this book)

Soil covering plant growth can prevent sealing due to sun-baking.

In some places it is common to burn organic waste material, or, even parts of the land surface to prepare it for planting. Ash is alkaline, and promotes plant growth, due to its composition, but burnt soil surface becomes nearly impenetrable for the water of the rainfalls that follow the first one after burning. By creating an ash water mix, initially, that has a waxy, water repelling characteristic, the wettability of soil gets reduced, promoting superficial runoff. This is another way soil can be sealed.

Another factor that leads to sealing of the soil, with long-term effects that are more difficult to cure, is the use of heavy machinery in huge agricultural operations. The problem is not only a superficial compaction that can be broken up again, but also a profound squeezing of the soil, diminishing its aeration and its pores, the ecological niche of microbiotic soil life. Each time a tractor or harvester rolls over the field has a negative compacting effect. The effect becomes devastating, as it accumulates with the years, and seals the deep part of the soil, creating impermeable layers that lead to waterlogging.

4. **Light sensitive plants should be shaded.**

Especially in the tropics, direct sunlight can be quite devastating for seedlings and light sensitive plants. This is why you should have your seedlings initially shaded by trees, hedges or taller plants. If you have a healthy mix of plants, instead of a monoculture, this is not much of an issue.

What works perfect are moringa trees (*Moringa oleifera*). They are not too tall and create a light shadow, leaving enough sunlight pass through their foliage. They have taproots and thus don't hinder the development of your plantation. So, if possible, plant moringa trees in strategic places, wherever you need some shady protection.

Another possibility is to protect areas with sensitive crops and seedlings with special, garden-supply, shading sunscreen mats that you can hang over wooden or aluminum frames. This way, your plants are shaded, and they still have all they need to develop adequately. Usually, this kind of appliance is used in plant nurseries.

5. The soil should be organized in furrows or terraces.

The following technique has been successfully applied, already for millennia, by people all over the world.

If your land is on a slope, the furrows or terraces should be organized along the contour lines of the landscape. This way, you prevent loss of soil and humus through superficial water runoff, reduce the erosion of your soil uphill, and avoid unequal repartition of humus, nutrients or salts on your plot with an accumulation of it down the hill. You also keep the soil moist for a longer period of time.

Depending on the kind of cultivation, you can plant in the furrow or on the mound. The best thing to do is to plant two or more different vegetables or plants, one in the furrow and one on the mound. For example, you choose carrots for the mound and lettuce or spinach for the furrow.

The mounds can be covered with composting foil with recesses on the top of the mound for the plants you want to grow. This way, you avoid the growth of bad weeds close to your crops.

If you plant trees on a slope, you can create a "swallow's nest" like circle around the trunk, excavating uphill a semi-circle using the material excavated to refill the lower part. The downhill part should get stabilized with rocks, and the so created circle should be inclined slightly against the slope, to catch water and nutrients when there is a runoff, caused by rain or by irrigation.

6. The soil should never be under stagnant water long-term.

If you have a place with occasionally stagnant water, because you are situated in a sink, on a riverbed, or have underneath some impermeable soil layer (such as clay, for example), you should dig drainage ditches where the water can run off faster to diminish the time your plant roots are exposed to stagnant water. This helps you to avoid damage in your plants caused by putrefaction, induced by stagnant water, especially in the root system.

Another point to take into consideration is that stagnant water very often leads to over acidification and salination of the soil. Plants sensitive to soil acidity and salts will wither away.

7. The soil should be checked for its composition and its pH. Deviations and deficiencies should be corrected, if necessary.

Plants need macronutrients (nitrogen, phosphorus, potassium, calcium and magnesium) and micronutrients (iron, manganese, copper, zinc, boron, molybdenum and aluminum) for healthy growth. The availability of these compounds depends highly on the pH of the soil. In a range between 5.5 and 7, most macronutrients are absorbable and unbound in complex compounds. When pH is lower than 6, phosphorus starts forming insoluble compounds with iron (Fe) and aluminum (Al), and when the pH is higher than 7, phosphorus starts forming insoluble compounds with calcium (Ca).

This is why control of the pH is essential for healthy plant growth.

To be sure that the essential nutrients are present in sufficient amounts, it makes sense to make a complete analysis to know the actual state of the soil. You should at least measure the main nutrients, or macronutrients, of your soil.

Unbalanced use of artificial mineral fertilizers mainly containing soluble nitrogen may lead to an acidification of the soil and, therefore, should be avoided.

You should be aware of the fact that each plant has an optimum pH range where it grows best. Some need rather acidic environments while others need neutral, or even alkaline, soil conditions.

When the pH is below 5.3 or above 6.8, a pH corrective action is indicated. There are always possibilities to correct the soil pH.

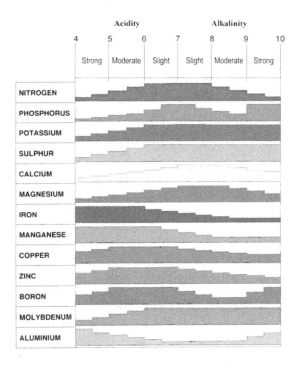

The graph shows the bioavailability of basic mineral plant nutrients at different pH levels.

In case the soil pH is above 6.8, the easiest way to correct the acidity is to reduce the pH of the soil by adding nitric acid (during growth phase) or phosphoric acid (during flowering phase) to the irrigating water. In case it is below 5.3, you should use potassium hydroxide (caustic potash) or potassium bicarbonate to increase the pH to desired values.

There are some few plants that need a more extreme soil pH. In these cases, you have to adjust the pH to their demands to have an abundant harvest.

8. **You should always mix different plants in clusters or rows; try companion planting and crop rotation. Diversification**

A way to prevent plagues is to avoid extended periods of pure monoculture. If you cultivate different plants in clusters or in alternating rows, you strengthen the natural, synergetic self-defense mechanisms. You will have a lot less problems with plagues.

Another advantage of mixed cultures is that, even if one of your cultivations suffers from a plague, you still have other vegetables that are unaffected, and, thus, you have less loss of income. You should also mix perennial plants with short-cycle plants, and taller growing with lower growing plants.

Whenever you eliminate the planting of one kind of plant after harvesting, prepare the soil to seed another kind of vegetable immediately.

Mixed cultures also prevent large areas of adjoining land from being bare at the same time after harvesting.

You should always alternate different plants on the same piece of land to avoid repetition. Thus, you avoid unbalanced consumption of nutrients and persistence of specialized plagues. This is why, in Europe in the Middle Ages, farmers used the three-field-system of crop rotation.

One field was planted in the autumn with winter wheat or rye; the second field was planted with other crops such as peas, lentils, or beans; and the third was left fallow, in order to allow the soil of that field to regain its nutrients.

The clusters and the amount of rows of the same plant depend on your decision, the size of your plot, and whether or not you are a commercial producer or just produce for private family consumption.

The cluster concept should also be applied to fruit tree plantations and even for the timber industry.

The more diverse the planting, the better the pest prevention and other synergetic effects that raise the overall productivity of your land.

However, be aware that not all plant combinations induce synergetic effects that are as positive as the "Indian Triple"-

corn, beans and squash-or the classic combination of tomatoes and carrots. Onions and garlic combined with beans, for example, diminish the growth of the latter. The more diverse the plantation, the better.

This approach is practiced in rural communities in Middle and South America, known as "Chakras Agricolas Integrales" very successfully. Plots that, cultivated the commercial way, didn't produce enough to sustain a family, now, create even a modest income, using the zoning and diversification of the produce, as is part of the concept of the "Chakras Integrales".

This might be a viable approach worthwhile to investigate.

9. You should always have leguminous plants in your plant assortment.

Leguminous plants are plants that live in symbiosis with the nitrate-accumulating bacteria rhizobiaceae. Present around the roots of leguminous plants, the rhizobia have the ability to bind elemental molecular nitrogen (N_2) by reducing it to ammonia (NH_3) and ammonium (NH_4 +), thus making it bioavailable to the plants.

For example, all kinds of beans, peas, clovers, peanuts, and the moringa tree are all leguminous plants. In fact, there are tens of thousands of species belonging to this vast plant family.

Alternating every now and then with plants from this family, or planting them in-between your plantings, nourishes your soil with bio-accessible nitrogen. This is, besides phosphorus, potassium, sulfur and calcium, the most important nutrient for healthy plant growth.

10. Give the plants enough space and sunlight.

You should give the plants enough space to develop adequately. This means growing the plants not too close to each other, but also not in a way that wastes space. According to mini-farming techniques, you can pack more plants per unit than usually done by commercial farmers. Each plant species has different requirements concerning density, soil, water and light.

Wasted space is space lost for the growing of food crops while allowing bad weeds to grow. It is also unused soil that is exposed to erosion, or has to be covered by foils or other means, like banana leaves or palm leaves.

You can look at your plantation as if there are three or four height-levels of plants. There are the low-growing, like onions, carrots and lettuce. There is the second level with taller plants, such as tomatoes or peppers, followed by the taller ones, such as yucca or eggplant. And, finally, the highest ones, such as fruit trees, plantains and bananas. All these plants with different heights have, also, different requirements for sunlight. So, you should choose a combination of different heights and use the areas shaded by tall growing crops for lower growing plants that require less sunlight.

You also can grow climbing plants, such as tayota or passion fruit, on artificial stands of ropes or wires and, below, have a carpet of low growers.

This way, you can learn to create a three-dimensional model for the use of the space above the soil.

Also note that you should plant the higher growing crops on the north side of your lot, if you live in the northern hemisphere, and vice versa, if you live in the southern hemisphere. On the equator, it doesn't matter much.

Be aware that plants grown too close together become stunted with little leaves and fruit.

11. The fertilizers used should be from a natural source.

Natural fertilizers should be given preference over artificial mineral fertilizers, most importantly because, using mineral fertilizers, we cannot call our products ecological, and even less, organic.

Mineral fertilizers don't stay in the soil. They wash out fast and, thus, endanger our groundwater, because they basically consist of water soluble salts, whereas natural fertilizers consist of more complex compounds of nutritive value.

Also, the bioavailability of artificial mineral fertilizers, due to its saline and water soluble nature, is much lower than organically bound natural fertilizing biomolecules produced by the microorganisms in humus-rich, healthy soil.

Chicken manure, cow dung or compost, as well as the draining water from a biodigestor or water from a fishpond, are much better alternatives. The various (as opposed to the single, isolated substances in mineral fertilizer) plant nutrients they contain are bound in insoluble compounds and are released slowly over the course of the time, according to the needs of the plant, without endangering the groundwater.

Natural fertilizers contain the most important plant nutrients, usually in a healthy mix, but, nevertheless, you should fertilize according to your soil composition and quality.

Combine, preferably, solid fertilizers with liquid ones, like cow dung or horse manure with water from a fish pond.

Solid fertilizers should be mixed with the soil when it is being prepared for planting. Liquid fertilizers should be administered with the irrigation system during the growth phase of the plants.

Healthy humus management reduces the need for fertilizers considerably and is the basis of Sustainable Ecological Organic Agriculture (SEOA). The important point is that the amount of organic material in the soil, which is decomposed by microorganisms and by natural biochemical processes to provide balanced plant nutrition, gets replaced by enough new organic material.

If the soil is naked, and you deprive it of dead leaves and decaying plants, it loses the fertility usually created by the continuous decomposition of present organic material. If the humus balance is negative, soil loses fertility. Organic waste is the food that millions of invisible microorganisms use as their energy source, and, while digesting the organic compounds, these microorganisms create plant available essential nutrients. The more soil life, the more fertile the ground.

Another important function of organic particles is that they store nutrients and prevent them from being washed out by the rain.

To replace the organic material consumed continuously, you need to plow in organic material after harvesting when you prepare the vegetable bed for the next seed. You can use solid fertilizers at first, as well as straw or dried and triturated plant material. Your aim should be to build up the amount of humus, by using organic material from different sources, to create an ever healthier mix and higher percentage of humus.

This is the place to mention green manure: You can have a separate field for producing fast growing plants that you harvest to plow under whenever a piece of your land is being prepared for a new production cycle. Beware that, in the tropics, the decomposition process can be much faster than in moderate climates due to a higher microbiotic turnover, depending on the average temperature.

The amount of fertilizer should be adapted to the consumption of different nutrients by the plants you harvest.

You should fertilize only during the growth phase of the plant, especially at the beginning and when the plant is flowering. While, during the winter time or times of withdrawal, the plant doesn't need nutrients. During these times, you should avoid fertilizing additionally.

Another point to be mentioned is foliate fertilizing. Usually, this kind of fertilizing is used to overcome acute nutrient deficiency occurring, especially, during drought.

Nutrients such as urea, and other water soluble, nonpolar substances (Chelates), reach the plant via diffusion through the leaves. This is why this kind of fertilization should be applied in the evening hours, because a water film on the leaves is necessary for this process. The dew helps to extend the assimilation phase.

Even under healthy soil conditions, this is a suitable additional option for Sustainable Ecological Organic Agriculture to raise quality and yield of your harvest.

To raise your soil's capacity to accumulate and hold on to nutrients, and to host more microorganisms, you can do what the natives of the Amazonas region did hundreds of years ago.

They created patches of black fertile soil, known as "Terra Preta do Indio", where they grew their crops in a sustainable way, in the middle of the poor surrounding soil of the rainforest, using charcoal.

As we know, activated coal is used in water filters to hold on to all the contaminants dissolved in the water. In the same way, coal holds on to all the nutrients in the soil and releases them according to the needs of the plants.

But, be aware, the surface area of the charcoal is ten thousand fold bigger than of any other material, which means, that, if you don't load it (soak it with nutrients) before mixing it with your soil, the existing nutrients will initially cling to it and, thus, reduce plant availability. Once loaded, it will serve as nutrient stock for years to come.

Soils enriched with coal produced in charcoal kilns also contain a lot more microbiotic life than soils that don't contain coal due to the pores that offer living spaces.

Producing charcoal whenever you have wood waste or any other dry organic waste, can be a means for you to enrich your soil, considerably. You just have to crush or grind the coal and load it with nutrients before mixing it with your soil.

12. Apply vermiculture

Earthworms, as part of soil life, are like industrial converters, turning organic matter into perfect fertile humus while eating their way through the ground. The more earthworms you have, the better the conversion of your organic, undigested matter into plant available stable macroclusters of nutrients.

Additionally, the worms loosen up the soil and create worm gears (the tunnels a worm creates while eating its way through the soil), offering living spaces for all kinds of soil-enriching organisms and room for roots. This way, they help to ameliorate soil texture and sponge function. Worm castings (the manure of worms) are highly fertile for organically enriched soil.

You can investigate your worm population by digging into your soil and observing how many worms you find in one shovel.

To raise your conversion rate, you can even apply vermiculture and transform, in particular, your kitchen waste directly into highly nutritive worm manure.

You can create boxes with worms which you feed with the right mix of organic waste, and your harvest will be worms and fertile organic dung.

In tropical and subtropical soils, worm population is less than in temperate climates, whereas the population of ants is much higher. Both do more or less the same job. So don't be worried if you don't find many worms. Ants are usually always around.

13. Produce your own biol

A good way to enrich your soil with predigested nutritive compounds for plants is with the production of your own biol.

Biol is the final product of an anaerobic fermentation process usually performed by bacteria.

To prepare a biol-fertilizer of your own, you need a hermetically sealed tank or barrel. You also need, on top of the tap, a valve connected to a hose that ends in a bottle filled with water, to eliminate the gas produced in the process of fermentation.

Fresh manure, which can be from different herbivores and shredded plants, such as alfalfa, guava, banana plant, and nettle leaf, as well as other organic waste, needs to be mixed with water and ground egg shells or bone meal to add the necessary inorganic component. Some milk and/or molasses, added to the mix sealed in your tank, kick starts the digestion process, necessary to concentrate and potentiate the fertilizing, growth-promoting compounds and to make the nutrients bioavailable. After about 30 days, you can harvest the content of your barrel, filter it and use it in diluted form as foliate or liquid fertilizer and as a health and growth-promoting additive to your irrigation water.

The recommended compositions and proportions vary a lot.

My advice is to collect some information about biol production, from the internet or other sources, and to experiment with your own means and mixtures.

The effectiveness of biol is only partly due to the nutrients concentrated in it; a big part of the effect is triggered by fito-cytokines, universal proteins that are responsible for resistances and gene-activation, amongst others.

There are endless combinations of supportive ingredients possible. Just create your own biol based on literature and your own research and experience.

According to my experience, biol, made from leafs of *Moringa oleifera,* is very effective in raising the immunity. Combined with biol from leafs from *Azaridachta indica* (Neem tree) it strengthens the plants and eliminates all common airborne plagues.

14. Create a fishpond to produce your own liquid fertilizer.

A way to create another continuous fertilizer source, plus an additional income source, is the creation of a fish tank or pond, preferably with Tilapia, a kind of carp which is a common fish filet. Other species you can use are different kinds of catfish.

Tanks are easier to handle than ponds. The water from the tank can be used directly or indirectly as irrigating water. This way, the nitrous-rich feces nourish the plants directly. The water taken out of the tanks for irrigation just needs to be replaced, which has to be done anyway.

The money you invest into additional fertilizers is better invested in organic fish feed. This way, you can kill two birds with one stone, or in other words, you will have two benefits. You have a natural fertilizer for your plants and you harvest fish that you can sell. Your investment pays back twice, in fruit and in fish.

If you have a spacious terrain with the possibility to create a natural pond to hold back runoff rainwater and to create a natural biotope, you additionally raise the biodiversity of your place, and you can have the same benefit of the fish tanks, only in a somehow more diluted and natural version.

It is much more problematic to have chickens to use their manure as fertilizer, because they usually have a lower efficiency coefficient. Also, if held as free running livestock, they endanger your plantings, because they consume any green they can find, especially your small green plant seedlings.

15. All organic waste material should be used to create humus. Create a compost heap.

As already stated above, a healthy humus production, by composting all kinds of organic material, is crucial for a successful organic operation.

Humus, the carbonic-organic decaying material in the soil that serves many purposes - from being a reservoir for nutrients and water to being a habitat for an endless army of microorganisms which promote healthy soil life - has to be renewed continuously.

We are harvesting our products and, in this way, diminishing the amount of nutrients in the soil. Creating humus out of all organic waste material that accumulates on the site, and in the kitchen, is essential for keeping an even humus balance, or even raising its percentage.

It even makes sense to grow fast-growing, nitrate-rich plants as organic material on wastelands to be shredded every now and then and used as "green manure", or for composting. Alfalfa, mustard and moringa are just some examples.

All this extra organic matter, if not used as green manure, and all coarse garden waste should be shredded and transformed into humus in a composting site. You should mix all organic kitchen waste with this shredded trash to have a healthy mix of shredded wood chops, twigs, leaves, rotten fruit, horse manure, straw, etc. You should not use meat or slaughterhouse leftovers, although they would decompose just as well in a compost site, because they also could attract wild dogs, rats and other unwanted guests.

Either, you mix in the half-rotten materials to provide raw food for the soil microbes, or you prepare a fully-rotten compost to be mixed with the soil. Combining both is the best way to have good results in building up soil that is rich in humus.

To create a composting site, you should pile up this material on a flat surface and cover it with special composting foil. The foil allows the transpiration of water and gases necessary for the composting process. Within 10-14 weeks, depending on the handling, around 60-70% of the material is broken down. This is when it can be mixed with the soil to raise the humus content. Another possibility is to wait longer, until the material is converted into finished compost fertilizer, and mix it as fertilizer with the soil before planting. The material from the compost heap can be enriched with other natural fertilizers and charcoal, before mixing it with your soil, ahead of planting.

Be aware that the degradation process can occur much faster in the tropics, due to the temperature and the microorganisms, than in temperate zones.

There are different ways of composting that get the same results. It is important to ventilate the compost enough. This means that you need to turn it over once or twice in the process, or you can use prefab composting containers.

The garden waste components, such as wood chips and twigs, should not be bigger than your fingers. They should be mixed with leaves or other kinds of organic material. The more diverse the mix is, the better the result.

During the initial composting process, the temperature rises naturally, for more than 2 weeks, to values above 60° C, and, thus, kills most of the opportunist and pathogen microorganisms that could cause pests if distributed on your fields before the composting process is finished. After the "hot phase", the temperature of the compost declines and permits the helpful microorganisms to multiply. This is when the compost is finished and can be used as concentrated humus fertilizer to be mixed with your upper soil layer. This should be done before planting.

16. Create an intelligent irrigating system.

If your lot is not too big, it is best to use an elevated water tank for your irrigation system. You can create a multiple pipe adapter system so that you can irrigate different parts of your lot individually, depending on the connections you open for the flow. The elevated tank should be in the middle of your land, so that the pipes or hoses are organized in a star shape, starting from the tank.

If you use a cistern or a direct pipe from a source, you always need a working water pump. Whereas, if you have an elevated water tank, you fill it with the pump and irrigate with just the force of gravity. This is the more convenient and functional way to water the plants. You just have to be sure that the water in the tank doesn't heat up during the daytime, so that you don't irrigate your plants with hot water. This is why such a tank should be covered and shaded by treetops, or protected by isolating walls and a roof.

Using an elevated water tank, you also can add any liquid fertilizer or supplement more easily and exactly.

Just note that, if you work with a sprinkler system, you need more pressure, and, thus, you need a pump or naturally high pipe pressure, and therefore you cannot work with an elevated tank.

17. Irrigate the plants in the morning and / or evening hours.

Irrigation should occur in the morning and/or in the evening hours to avoid too much loss of water through evaporation, and to avoid burning the leaves.

Water drops on leaves and fruit can act as a glass lens, concentrating the sunbeams in a way that causes harm by heating up and burning the leaves. This happens especially when irrigating with a sprinkler system during the daytime.

The water in the above ground, typically black, irrigating tubes can heat up to boiling temperatures in plain sun. This is why you should not irrigate in the daytime: to not harm the sensitive roots of your plants and the microorganisms in your soil.

Big temperature differences between the irrigating water and the sun-heated soil should be avoided. This leads to a kind of shock state and diminishes the growth rate.

All these points mentioned above are the reasons why early morning, or late evening, irrigation is the most effective.

Although, evening hours are to be preferred, because moist at night time induces dew creation, whereas the moist in the morning evaporates in the rising heat of the day.

Be also aware that a plant needs more water while in its growth phase than during the ripening phase of the fruit or tubercle. You should adapt your irrigation scheme to this fact, too, as you adapt the fertilization of the plants the same way.

18. Grow according to the necessities of the plants.

Depending on your present quality of soil, you should plant the types of plants that grow well based on these actual circumstances. With the time it takes to raise the humus content and quality of the soil, you will be able to plant whatever you want to grow.

In the areas that are rather shady, grow plants that don't need full sunlight and, in exposed sunny areas, grow plants that require exposure to sun.

If you have wet depressions, you should use these areas for plants that need much water and dry hill slopes for plants that can stand dry soil, or even require it.

In fact, there is no bad soil! There is just the wrong selection of plants to grow in the wrong soil.

Dry and stony alkaline soil, or sandy, wet, acidic soil, offers a completely different initial situation. The more extreme the soil conditions are, the less variety of plants you can choose from, because fewer plants are adapted to these extreme conditions. So, your aim should be to create healthy, balanced soil conditions that make the growth of a wider range of varieties of plants possible.

This means that you should learn about the plants you want to grow and select them carefully, so that you are not disappointed with the result at the beginning.

With time, while your soil management leads to a rise in humus-organic-carbon content and to a structural improvement of your site, you will be ever more able to grow a wider range of plants and fruit.

19. Protect your plantation with windbreaks and hedge trees.

Wind can be quite destructive to your plantings in several ways. It can uproot and overthrow the plants during a thunderstorm or a cyclone. If your piece of land is flat, and there is no windbreak, it also can dry the surface of the soil quite fast, carry away valuable soil components, and, thus, lead to silent erosion of your plot.

This is why wind-shielding hedges and rows of trees, especially at the side of your lot where the wind usually comes from, are very important.

The wind-shielding effect depends mostly on the height of the trees: their height, multiplied by approximately 15, gives you the distance behind the trees that is shielded when the wind comes parallel to the terrain. This means that if you have a row of 10 m tall fruit trees, you shield a distance of up to 150 m behind this tree row from destructive wind forces.

The tree row usually leaves some wind to pass through the stems. To reduce this effect, you can plant bushes or small fruit trees below the tall ones. This way, you create maximum protection. As trees create shadows, you should select shade-loving plants for the areas north of the tree rows.

There are also some cactus-like spurges or bamboo that can be used as natural green fencing to avoid the wind that dries out the soil and blows it away. Also, they grow so thick that such a natural fence even serves to keep intruders out.

20. When you eliminate plants, replace them with others.

Whenever you harvest or remove a plant, a cluster, or a field, you should replace it with another plant after digging over and, eventually, fertilizing with compost or dung. This way, the soil is not uncovered for long, and you make maximum use of your land.

To avoid unbalanced leaching of the soil, you should change the plant species every now and then. Some leguminous species should be included in your selection, in between some cycles, to enrich the soil with nitrates produced by its symbiotic root bacteria.

If you cut down a tree, you should plant another one, as long as the elimination of the tree was not just a means to create more light and air for your vegetable plantings.

21. Prune plants and trees extensively.

Well-pruned fruit trees produce much more fruit than unpruned ones, because having a lot of wild shoots consumes a lot of energy. A pruned tree uses more energy to form fruit than an unpruned one, which produces wild shoots and unproductive growth.

The method of pruning depends on the kind of tree. A lemon tree needs different pruning than a mango tree or an avocado tree. Look it up and collect your own experience. Pruning is a science on its own.

Pruning the trees accordingly also makes the collection of the fruit easier.

But be careful, though, not to eliminate grafted branches.

22. Natural pest control.

The fact that, nowadays, lots of insecticides and pesticides are used in industrial and commercial agriculture to control eventual diseases and pests has led to a decrease in insects. This has been followed subsequently by a decrease in predators, such as birds and lizards. Because of this, the natural balance has been disturbed. The process of impoverishing nature must be stopped in order to have efficient, natural pest control.

This is why it makes sense, if you have enough space, to create isles of natural, wild growing vegetation, shrubs and trees. Thus, you create a place where a wide variety of plants, insects, lizards and other wildlife, even bats, can withdraw.

Another way to integrate nature for pest control is to subdivide your parcel with wild growing hedges.

Have you ever heard of "Insect-Hotels"? This is another way to invite a great variety of helpful wasps and bees into your garden. Just leave dead trees standing or take some trunks and drill holes of different sizes into it. You will see that soon they will be inhabited.

The pesticides affect not only the harmful insects, but also the useful ones, such as bees and all the other insects that pollinate our crops and fruit trees. Without these helpful insects, our harvest would be very low. We owe our abundant production to them, and this should be a reason to pamper, instead of eliminate, them.

Another reason to stop, or at least drastically diminish, the use of pesticides is the fact that we are at the end of the food chain. Plants and animals store non-biodegradable and long-term, persistent, complex chemical substances, which are used as pest control and are partly known to cause cancer and other health problems, passing it along the food chain until we find them in the food we buy in the supermarket. Long-forbidden pesticides, such as DDT, are still found in polar bears in Greenland and in penguins in Patagonia, where this pesticide was never used.

Every plant species has its own diseases and pests that they are susceptible to.

Diseases and pests occur especially in monocultures and in plantings that are subjected to massive chemical fertilization. These methods of agriculture weaken the natural defense systems of the plants.

Nowadays, we have ever more often climatic stress factors, such as unnaturally pronounced phases of drought or inundations, which make the plants susceptible to pests due to a weakening of their immune system.

Pests and diseases are species-specific. If a monoculture becomes affected, all your harvest is in danger. The Colorado potato beetle, for example, only affects potatoes, but it will not harm any other crop or vegetable. If you have potatoes, corn, plantains and yucca in a healthy, mixed culture, the probability that all your potatoes will be affected is less than if you had a monoculture.

Mixed cultures with a broad assortment of different plants suffer a lot less from diseases and pests. A 10% loss of production due to some pest in a healthy ecosystem is normal and shouldn't bother us.

If some plants, bushes, or trees get sick, eliminate and burn them and replace them with other plants. This is easier and faster than hoping to overcome a disease. Try different varieties of plants to find resistant ones that fit into your "portfolio". And don't forget: never change a winning team unless it is starting to lose.

If you have a plague of insects or their larvae, you can use very effective organic extracts, from the Neem tree for example. These extracts should be applied directly to the leaves and in the irrigation water.

If you have problems with slugs, you just need some ducks.

If you have problems with mice or rats, you need some cats.

There is nearly always a solution to any threat that comes up, because each pest has its own natural enemies that we can use. Once the pest is overcome, natural balance is usually restored.

As pests usually are very selective and only feast on a specific host, as already mentioned above, by removing the host (not planting the host plant) for a period longer than the full life cycle of the pest, we can get rid of them.

This unfortunately doesn't work with some obdurate mildew caused by fungi that persist for a longer period of time, as spores or mycelium, in the soil. As those are also quite species-specific, just avoid growing the plants that are affected by the mildew that your soil is contaminated with, or look for resistant types.

When do diseases and pests usually attack? When your plants are feeble and have weak immune systems. This means that the most important part of disease prevention and pest control is having healthy plants. You can achieve this with proper soil and water management, correct fertilization and a healthy assortment of plants.

You can also use natural immune boosting extracts from different plants, such as moringa, that supplement other substances, such as plant-cytokines, that help to raise the defense system of the plants and, thus, avoid, or at least diminish, the impact of diseases and pests.

Again, these extracts should be applied to the leaves and via the irrigation water. It is always better to prevent pests, by acting wisely in maintaining healthy and resistant plants based on proper soil and water management, than to react to plagues with natural or chemical means.

23. Install beehives.

If your lot is big enough to install beehives in one corner, you shouldn't hesitate. They help to pollinate most of your crops and fruit trees, and they produce healthy, delicious honey as a secondary benefit. Without honey bees and bumblebees around your plantings, your fruit harvest would be lower than it could be, because most fruit trees need bees for pollination. Other insects usually can't successfully accomplish this task.

Of course, there are plants that get along without bees, because they have adapted in some way: they have symbiotic relationships with other pollinizers that they have created in the course of evolution, they get pollinated by the wind, or they are hermaphrodites. Cacao flowers, for example, get pollinated by a special kind of tiny fly, whereas coffee plants need bees.

You don't need to become a beekeeper; you can look for someone with bees and ask him to put his hives on your site. This way, you don't have to assume responsibility, but you will benefit.

24. Try "Electroculture"

As early as the 18th century, when modern electricity and its uses were explored, a branch of "electroculture", a kind of application of electric currents in agriculture, arose.

There are very interesting and promising research results around, with up to more than a 100% increase in production, using this methods.

As all living organisms manifest measurable electric phenomena, and our atmosphere is loaded with a static electric field that, although we don't perceive it, seems to be essential in the development of plant life, we should consider looking at this option to improve our harvest, as it is naturally beneficial.

To prove the importance of this static electric field, we just have to try growing plants in a faraday cage. They wither away within it.

You can try electroculture with the natural "Earth Battery", using just two electrodes of different materials, or you can try a more sophisticated approach, transforming solar patio lights into electrical sources, sending the current along a wire through the root system of your plants.

Be innovative and creative. It seems that using an old idea in a modern, new and organic way might help to improve your harvest.

25. Special Point: The rhythms of nature reflected by the influence of the moon.

For sure you have heard from your grandparents, or from other elderly people, about the right time to plant, according to the different phases of the moon. Throughout generations people have observed the influence of the moon on natural processes, such as the tides or the menstruation cycle. They also found some basic rules for successful agriculture, according to the four basic phases that the moon goes through within one month. Although modern science is doubtful, empiric experience confirms these ancient findings.

When the moon is increasing, or waxing, the juice of the plants ascends into the aboveground parts of the plant. Whereas, when the moon is decreasing, or waning, the sap concentrates into the belowground parts of the plants, especially the tubers and roots.

In the first quarter of the waxing moon, in which its light gradually becomes brighter, the natural growth processes in the aboveground parts of the plants increase. Therefore, you should seed, plant and take care of all plants you want to harvest the leaves or aboveground parts from in this phase. This is also the time to harvest these plants.

The second quarter of the waxing moon until the full moon should be dedicated to the fruit plants that develop aboveground. Again, this applies to setting, caretaking and harvesting. The creation of cuttings and the crafting of plants should also be done during this moon phase.

During the full moon, its power reaches its peak. It is time to fertilize gardens and fields, since the plants can absorb nutrients easily and effectively. You shouldn't prune trees during this time.

During the following moon phase, the energy of the plants withdraws into the ground, and underground growth is promoted. You should seed, plant and take care of root vegetables, bulbs, and tubers. As the juice of the trees concentrates in the roots, this is when they should be pruned.

As you can see, there are many interesting aspects which can be incorporated into daily practice.

Just observe these things on your own to approve or dismiss the ideas, but, according to my observations, these rules are very helpful in generating high yields from healthy plants.

26. Marketing concept, or, what to do with all your products.

If you work the organic way described in this book, your fruit and vegetable should have a high quality, are tastier than conventionally produced goods, and are loaded with vitamins and minerals, providing best quality for health conscious consumers.

The question, what to do with all the fruit and vegetable you produce in your garden or on your field doesn't arise, when you just produce for your own family-consumption.

But, if this is not the case, you have to think of how to market your harvest.

The most common way to sell your goods is the local fruit and vegetable market. This is the easiest and best way, if you have every now and then a harvest of different crops.

There are many ways to enter the market, either through personal relationships, or through a cooperative you can form part of. All depends on the variety and the amount you produce. Perhaps you have a bigger production that you can plan to supply supermarkets with.

If you have a wide variety of goods and a concept of continuous harvest, another quite lucrative way of marketing opens up to you. The advantage of the tropical and subtropical climate is the year round production. Thus, you can offer a subscription model with weekly delivery of a basket with fresh vegetables and fruits. You may vary in size and composition, according to the fee. You can add even finished products such as jam, dried fruits or herbal teas. This is a very flexible and worthwhile approach. With the time you can built up your clientele and you can plan your income. This concept works best when several small producers associate.

There is a growing population of health conscious consumers all over the world that welcome such a distribution system.

Go ahead with this idea and adapt it to your circumstances; there are already many working with it!

27. A personal tip.

After reading the concepts collected and displayed in this booklet, you may have a better understanding of the underlying concepts of **Sustainable Ecological Organic Agriculture**, a new and holistic approach to agriculture.

But, for sure, you will still have many unanswered and newly arisen questions, which, hopefully, motivate you to go deeper into the topic to improve your personal project.

Keep a diary to record all your observations, and, if something doesn't work out the way you tried it, change the strategy and compare the results.

There is always a way to improve. Don't worry if sometimes things don't work out as planned. There are so many factors involved, and you can control only the basic ones. But, if you are open to observing nature and learning continuously, and if you use healthy seeds and saplings and cling to the basic rules mentioned in this brochure, your work will be crowned with success, especially when you love what you do.

Learning this way, you find the best strategy in the framework of health-promoting Sustainable Ecological Organic Agriculture.

Once you are there, never change your winning strategy!

Always stay curious, and never stop searching for better solutions.

D. Basic tools:

The basic tools you need to run a small, self-sufficient garden or a lucrative, small farming business in tropical or subtropical climates, where you can harvest and grow all year-round are the following:

Just take this list as a guideline that you can adjust to your individual needs .

1. A (small) motorized **ROTARY TILLER** to dig over and loosen up the soil effectively, adapted to the size of your plot. (Or a tractor with different adjusted tools if the size of your enterprise requires it)
2. A (small) motorized **SHREDDER** to chop the organic waste for composting and producing green manure.
3. A (small) **WATER PUMP** to move the water into the elevated water tank or to create pressure in the pipes for irrigation.

4. A (small) **CHAINSAW** for cutting trees and pruning.
5. Different **SPADES, HOES** and **SHOVELS** for basic soil work and planting.
6. A **WHEELBARROW** and some **BUCKETS** for harvesting and any kind of transportation.
7. Different sizes of **DIBBLES** for seeding and planting.
8. Different **PRUNERS** for pruning.
9. A **MACHETE** for different purposes.
10. **COMPOSTING FOIL** to cover the compost or areas of soil.
11. **PLASTIC WATER TANKS (**to be elevated) with an irrigation pipe system for intelligent irrigation and for biol production.
12. **And, of course, all kinds of workshop and household tools for any need.**

If your operation is bigger, you will need more heavy machinery.

Dr. Oliver Pfaff

Fertile SOIL
is not just dirt

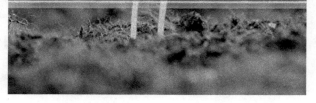

*A comprehensive and fascinating
introduction into this complex subject*

Oliver Pfaff

Just some thoughts...
about our daily bread

An entertaining, comprehensive, partly philosophical
approach to this complex and fascinating topic

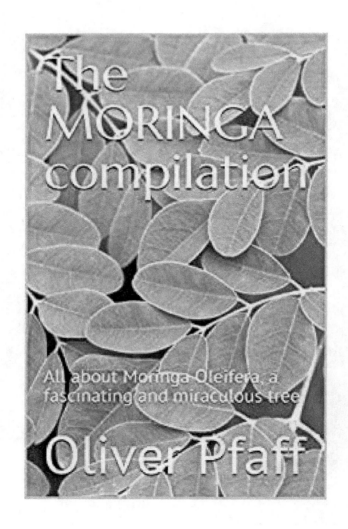

The MORINGA compilation

All about Moringa Oleifera, a fascinating and miraculous tree

Oliver Pfaff

9 781523 813506